For my sister, Anna. Thank you for your steadfast support.—A.S.

For my father, the adventurer, who trusted that I would find my own way.—S.W.

Consultancy by Henrietta Hammant

First published in 2025 in the United States of America by
Thames & Hudson Inc., 500 Fifth Avenue, New York, New York 10110

EU Authorized Representative: Interart S.A.R.L.
19 rue Charles Auray, 93500 Pantin, Paris, France
productsafety@thameshudson.co.uk
interart.fr

Library of Congress Control Number 2024932539

ISBN 978-0-500-65355-5
01

Printed and bound in China by C&C Offset Printing Co. Ltd

MIX
Paper | Supporting responsible forestry
FSC® C008047

RACE TO THE SOUTH POLE

THE BRITISH EXPEDITION

ALEXANDRA STEWART
SARAH WILKINS

t&h

ENTERING THE RACE

CAPTAIN SCOTT RECEIVES SOME BAD NEWS

Like a silent assassin, the telegram was waiting for Captain Robert Falcon Scott when he docked in the bustling port of Melbourne, Australia. Short, sharp, and brutally efficient, its words left Scott reeling in shock and not a little confusion.

BEG LEAVE TO INFORM YOU
FRAM PROCEEDING ANTARCTIC.

It was signed by Roald Amundsen, the world-famous Norwegian polar explorer. Amundsen—who was supposed to be on his way to the North Pole aboard his ship the *Fram*—was now heading in precisely the opposite direction!

During the seconds it took Scott to read the bombshell message, the tightly held dream—for which he was about to risk everything—began to slip from his grasp.

In just under two months, he and his team would sail their ship, the *Terra Nova*, into the icy waters of Antarctica. Their mission: a scientific study of the world's most mysterious continent and—the crowning glory—a do-or-die attempt to be the first men to reach the South Pole, on behalf of Great Britain.

But what Scott had assumed would be a battle between man and nature had just become a contest between two men, two teams, and two nations.

For Scott, the dream had started a decade earlier when, as a young officer in the Royal Navy, he had been picked to lead the British National Antarctic Expedition—the world's first major expedition to mainland Antarctica.

Setting off in 1901 aboard the Royal Research Ship *Discovery*, the party of seamen and scientists had spent two years exploring, measuring, and mapping the vast frozen wilderness.

During that time, Scott and two teammates—Edward "Bill" Wilson and Ernest Shackleton—had journeyed closer to the South Pole than anyone had ever been before. But sick with scurvy, starving, and broken, they had turned around 460 miles shy of their goal.

Hailed as heroes back home, they had fired the starting pistol on the race to reach the South Pole.

In 1908, Shackleton had made his own tantalizingly close attempt at reaching the Pole. Now, six years after he'd last set foot in Antarctica, Scott was returning to finish what he'd started. This was his race to win.

Betraying no emotion, Scott folded up the telegram and gritted his teeth. It was too late to change his carefully laid plans. There was nothing else he could do. They would just have to carry on as though Amundsen didn't exist.

ALL ABOARD!

SETTING SAIL ON THE *TERRA NOVA*

Just four months earlier, on a warm June day in 1910, the heavily laden *Terra Nova* had sailed proudly out of Cardiff Bay in Wales.

Gathered on deck, beaming and waving at the crowds of well-wishers lining the shoreline, was Scott's team: a multitalented cast of sailors, scientists, medics, officers, mechanics, and even a photographer. They had been selected from more than 8,000 applicants.

SHIP'S STORES

The *Terra Nova* was full to the brim with gear and supplies for the expedition, including ready-to-assemble timber huts, scientific instruments, photographic equipment, and three state-of-the-art motor sleds, which Scott believed would revolutionize polar exploration.

The men were divided into two groups: the "shore party" (thirty-three men), who would be dropped off in Antarctica, and the "ship's party" (thirty-two men), who would sail the *Terra Nova* back to New Zealand for the winter. If all went well, the ship would return to Antarctica in January 1912 to resupply the shore party, carry out further scientific work, and collect anyone who needed to go home.

The *Terra Nova* would make its long journey south by way of Madeira, South Trinidad, South Africa, Australia, and New Zealand, picking up more supplies and more colleagues along the way, most notably ponies and dogs.

ANIMALS ON BOARD

Once they reached New Zealand, the team took aboard nineteen Siberian ponies and thirty-three sled dogs to help them in Antarctica. These were paid for by British and New Zealand school children. Each school "gifted" their own animal. On the ship there was also a stowaway black cat—for whom the crew made a tiny hammock, blanket, and pillow—and a rabbit, brought aboard by an expedition member, Tom Crean.

TOM CREAN'S RABBIT

SHIP'S CAT

33 SLED DOGS

19 SIBERIAN PONIES

FOOD AND LUXURIES

While many items were essential for keeping everyone on the expedition fed, hydrated, and healthy, they weren't short of a few luxuries as well! Supplies included 162 carcasses of mutton, 150 gallons of lime juice (to ward off scurvy), 35,000 cigars, and half a ton of tobacco, and they even took a gramophone and a pianola for entertainment.

150 GALLONS OF LIME JUICE

GRAMOPHONE

PIANOLA

STORMY SEAS AHEAD

THE VOYAGE TO ANTARCTICA

The long journey southward aboard the cramped *Terra Nova* was a valuable time for the team to get to know one another. Officers, sailors, and scientists all cheerfully helped out, stoking the boilers and swabbing the decks. Not even the arrival of Amundsen's shocking news in Melbourne could puncture the lively mood.

On November 26, amid a blizzard of Union Jack flags and cheering crowds, the *Terra Nova* left New Zealand's Lyttelton Harbour on the last leg of its journey to Antarctica. The ship was now so crammed with men, animals, and cargo that it was sitting dangerously low in the water.

Three days after departing, a raging gale unleashed its fury. Winds shrieked through the rigging, while mountainous waves pounded the decks. Two ponies and a dog died in the chaos and the crew were forced to throw tons of precious fuel overboard to keep the overladen ship afloat.

To make matters worse, the ship's pumps became clogged, flooding the hull and putting the *Terra Nova* in grave danger of sinking. The men resorted to bailing the water out by hand.

Using just three iron buckets, they heaved and hauled, hour after hour. At long last, the pumps were fixed, the storm died down, and the water retreated. The men were exhausted, battered, but safe . . . for now.

Sailing onward, it wasn't long before they hit their next obstacle: the pack—a giant jigsaw of floating ice that guarded the Antarctic continent. With no way around it, the *Terra Nova* had to ram and barge its way through this menacing blockade. Yet the ice pieces were often so thick and tightly wedged together that the ship became trapped for days on end.

Finally, after three torturous weeks of stop and start, the *Terra Nova* emerged from the pack's steely grip and steamed into the open sea.

ARRIVAL IN ANTARCTICA

SETTING UP CAMP

The new year brought new excitement, with the first glimpse of the majestic Mount Erebus on the horizon. Two days later, the *Terra Nova* glided into McMurdo Sound—an icy bay between Ross Island and mainland Antarctica.

Mooring the ship to an ice floe, Scott spied a rocky headland at the foot of Erebus. It was the ideal place to establish their winter quarters—and he christened it "Cape Evans" in honor of his second in command, Edward "Teddy" Evans. Anxious to get ashore, the crew immediately began to unload their gear onto the ice.

The ponies whinnied and snorted with delight as their hooves touched firm ground for the first time in over a month. After a day's rest, they were put to work, hauling loads across the sea ice to base camp.

The dogs, motor sleds, and men hauled too, watched closely by curious groups of Adélie penguins and menacing packs of hungry killer whales. But catastrophe struck a few days later when one of the three motor sleds fell through the melting sea ice to a watery grave.

The crew unloaded the *Terra Nova* in just eight days and, on January 18, they moved into their newly built hut. Warm and inviting, with the gentle ticking and whirring of instruments in the scientists' corner and the smell of baking bread wafting from the oven, Scott marveled at the comfort of their new home.

But this was no time to relax. The Antarctic summer was slipping by and very soon darkness would descend upon them for four long months. They needed to use all the light that was left to prepare for next summer's "southern journey."

PREPARING THE WAY

DEPOT-LAYING MISSION

On January 24, 1911, Scott, twelve other men, eight ponies, and twenty-six dogs set out across the Great Ice Barrier, pulling tightly packed sleds. Their mission was to lay "depots"—stores of food and fuel—along a stretch of the route they would eventually take to the Pole. This was a crucial part of Scott's plan. They simply wouldn't be able to haul all the gear needed for the 1,800 mile round trip to the Pole in one go. Dropping some off in advance would solve this problem.

To Scott's dismay, there was trouble from the start. The ponies plunged and floundered through stretches of deep, soft snow. Then raging blizzards slowed the procession to a snail's pace.

As the ponies grew weaker and weaker, Scott became fearful they wouldn't survive the journey back to base. And so, 30 miles short of their intended destination, he made a fateful decision to dump their last load early. Naming this final stop "One Ton Depot" after the weight of stores they left there, the men built a tall snow tower—a cairn—as a marker and turned wearily for home.

Six ponies died during the return journey and all the animals were reduced to little more than fur and bones. In a heart-stopping moment, Scott feared he would lose some of the dogs too, when ten disappeared into a hidden crevasse—a deep crack in the ice—"like rats down a hole." Miraculously, after two hours of heaving, they managed to rescue the terrified animals. Drained and downcast, the men plodded onward, hoping that their trials were over for now.

But as the depot-laying party drew closer to Cape Evans, they received startling news from some teammates who had traveled across the ice to meet them. While out on an exploratory mission, the *Terra Nova* had stumbled across Roald Amundsen's ship, the *Fram*, moored to the Great Ice Barrier's edge in an area called the Bay of Whales.

Amundsen's base camp was just 400 miles east of Cape Evans—practically on their doorstep, in Antarctic terms. If that wasn't bad enough, it was 60 miles closer to the Pole than Cape Evans. "There is no doubt that Amundsen's plan is a very serious menace to ours," Scott confided in his diary.

A LONG, DARK WINTER

WORK AND LIFE AT CAPE EVANS

After the trials of the depot-laying journey, Scott and his team were heartily relieved to return to the reassuring surroundings of Cape Evans.

While they had been away, the rest of the shore party had been busy putting the finishing touches to their living quarters and settling into a brisk working routine.

There was much to do: from cooking and cleaning, to caring for the animals and battening down the hatches for the looming Antarctic winter.

There was also the important business of science to attend to. For Scott, scientific research was the key focus of the whole expedition. Consequently, everyone got involved in the painstaking work of measuring, recording, collecting, and observing everything around them. This included animals, rocks, weather, glaciers, ocean currents, and ice formations.

As if their task wasn't big enough, it was made all the tougher by the terrible conditions they had to operate in. Ice frosted up instruments and mercury froze in the thermometers. Snow clogged up equipment and flew into eyes, making it almost impossible to see anything, let alone take scientific readings. It was hard and often dangerous work. Even when the sun disappeared on April 23, ushering in four months of darkness, storms, and even lower temperatures, the work continued around the clock. No power on Earth could make the men abandon their scientific quest.

The science wasn't just confined to Cape Evans. Two teams, the northern and western parties, were sent on their own intrepid expeditions to explore other parts of Antarctica. Meanwhile, Bill Wilson, Henry "Birdie" Bowers, and Apsley Cherry-Garrard completed a reckless trip in the middle of winter to collect emperor penguin eggs. Dubbed "The Worst Journey in the World," they barely survived thirty-five horrific days in -70°F temperatures.

When the men weren't working, they filled their spare time with soccer matches on the ice, games of chess, checkers, and backgammon, reading, and lively discussions. They even created their own newspaper called *The South Polar Times*.

Scott also organized a program of evening lectures, during which the men took turns to speak about anything from rocks and rainbows to weather forecasting and the Great Wall of China.

On Midwinter's Day—the halfway point between Antarctica's last sunset and its next sunrise—the team celebrated with a feast, party games, and an enormous Christmas tree made from sticks, string, feathers, and colored paper. Outside the hut, nature marked the occasion in its own way, with a dazzling display of dancing aurora lights.

THE RACE BEGINS

STAGE ONE: THE GREAT ICE BARRIER

At last, the wait was over. Departure day dawned without fanfare on November 1, 1911. After breakfast, ten ponies led by ten men shuffled haphazardly off into the great white desert, dragging heavily laden sleds behind them. The speedy dog teams would follow on in a few days' time.

Ahead of them all were the slowest members of the expedition—the two motor sleds. These temperamental machines had sputtered off on October 24.

Scott had planned the journey with naval precision. Using Shackleton's polar journey as a guide, he'd calculated the entire 1,800 mile round trip would take 144 days.

But, of the sixteen men starting the journey, just one team of four would go all the way to the Pole. The rest were there to transport the food and provisions the final team needed to get to the Pole . . . and back.

One by one, the supporting teams would drop their supplies at depots and turn for home, leaving just three lucky men to accompany Scott for the final stretch to the Pole. He would only decide who his teammates would be at the final moment.

The animals and machines, however, would only go as far as the Beardmore Glacier because Scott didn't think they would make it up the crevasse-riddled ice. As the ponies weakened, they would be shot for food (feeding men and dogs). The final few would be killed at the bottom of the glacier and, from that point onward, the men would drag the sleds themselves.

To begin with, the pony teams made steady progress, covering around 12 miles a day. They marched at night so that the ponies could rest when the sun was high in the sky and the temperatures were warmer.

Yet, despite the summer season, the weather was unpredictable. On one day, the sun's glare would scorch the men's faces and burn their eyes; on another, powerful winds and heavy snow would leave them stumbling and slipping blindly southward.

Scott's mood brightened and darkened in harmony with the sky. But not even the sun's cheerful rays could blot out his disappointment when the team came across a broken and abandoned motor sled on November 4.

Two days later, they found the second with a note saying that the motor teams were continuing on foot. "So, the dream of great help from the machines is at an end!" Scott wrote.

Better news arrived the next day in the form of the dog teams. They had managed to travel at lightning speed across the Barrier, despite a punishing snowstorm.

STUCK IN THE SNOW

THE GATEWAY TO THE GLACIER

The marching continued across the Barrier's frozen wasteland—hard, dull, and disorienting. As the sky and snowy plain merged before them, it felt like they were walking into a great wall of white.

On November 21, the ponies caught up with the two man-hauling motor teams. Three days later, one of those teams—Hooper and Day—turned for home. On this day, too, Scott ordered their weakest pony, Jehu, to be shot and fed to the ravenous dogs.

Just over a month into their journey, the men at last caught a glimpse of the mighty Beardmore Glacier. They were now just 12 miles from the "Gateway," a steep snow slope that would take them safely from the Barrier up onto the great tumbling river of ice. The first stage of their journey was almost over.

But, as if on cue, a fierce blizzard swept in, pinning them down in their tents as it raged on for four days and four nights. Already behind schedule, and with rations running low, Scott flickered between misery and desperation.

Finally, on December 9, the wind dropped and the men emerged, blinking, from the tents to begin digging everyone and everything out of the thick, wet snow. Later that day, they moved off at a grinding crawl. After twelve hours of solid slog, they were nearly at the top of the Gateway. Exhausted but relieved, they stopped to camp. Here, the five remaining ponies were shot.

"We were thankful to rest, but more thankful still that we need drive those weary ponies no more," Cherry-Garrard later recalled. "It was a horrid business, and the place was known as Shambles Camp."

DAILY RATIONS FOR ONE MAN

16 ounces (450 g) biscuits*
12 ounces (340 g) pemmican**
3 ounces (85 g) sugar
2 ounces (57 g) butter
0.7 ounces (20 g) tea
0.6 ounces (16 g) cocoa

The men also ate fresh pony meat when it was available.

These daily rations provided around 4,500 calories. We now know that dragging heavy sleds at high altitude requires at least 6,000 calories a day. Scott's team were only eating three quarters of what they needed.

*The biscuits were high in protein content and very hard.

**Pemmican is an energy-rich meat mix invented by Indigenous people in North America. Scott's pemmican combined ground meat and fat. It was usually made into "hoosh," a thick soup of meat and melted snow. Crushed biscuits, arrowroot powder, curry powder, and raisins were often added to the hoosh to thicken it and provide flavor.

ONWARD AND UPWARD

STAGE TWO: THE BEARDMORE GLACIER

Tumbling 7,200 ft. downward from the Polar Plateau, the Beardmore Glacier is a 125 mile-long labyrinth of ice, where one wrong turn can spell death. If the Great Ice Barrier had been challenging, it was merely a warm-up for what was to come.

Hauling their heavy loads through this treacherous maze would have been daunting enough, but the blizzard had made it tougher still. Scott and his team were forced to plow thigh-high through soft, thick snow. The sleds dragged like lead and constantly toppled over. What's more, lurking beneath the snow, waiting to swallow them up at any moment, were countless crevasses.

The work was backbreaking and, now that the men had switched back to day-marching, it was performed under the glaring rays of the summer sun. Sweat poured off the men's bodies and faces, soaking their clothes and fogging up their goggles. Anyone who removed their eye protection in the hope of seeing their way was soon struck by snow blindness. Trudging upward "as blind as a bat," Birdie Bowers confided in his diary that he had been "enduring the pains of hell with my eyes."

TAKING A TUMBLE

DANGER ON THE GLACIER

A day and a half into their glacier journey, the men built another depot and the dog teams turned for home. Scott had already taken them much further than he'd originally intended. So, with dog food supplies running low and uncertainty up ahead, the time had come for them to return.

The remaining men were now on their own, dragging sleds heavier than grand pianos. They were about five days behind Shackleton's timeline and the going was so slow that on one day they gained just half a mile in nine hours!

By now, everyone's faces were burned to a crisp, and their lips were raw and blistered. They were plagued by thirst and reduced to chipping up ice as they marched—only drinking when they stopped for a break. Somehow though, they picked up their pace and still found time to photograph, sketch, and measure the glacier, as well as examine its rocks.

Finally, on December 21, the men climbed wearily onto the Polar Plateau—but not before they had all taken a tumble into a crevasse!

"The Lord only knows how deep these vast chasms go down," Bowers recorded. "They seem to extend into blue-black nothingness thousands of feet below."

But, for Scott, the terror of dangling into an abyss was eclipsed by the sheer relief of reaching the summit with enough rations to take them onward to the Pole.

"We ought to get through," he wrote before turning in for a well-deserved rest.

MARCHING ON

STAGE THREE: THE POLAR PLATEAU

The men's joy at arriving on the Polar Plateau was tinged with sadness. The time had come to wave farewell to another sled team. After helping to lay the Upper Glacier Depot, Atkinson, Wright, Keohane, and Cherry-Garrard turned reluctantly northward.

With no time to dwell on their teammates' disappointment, the remaining sled parties gritted their teeth and marched onward and upward.

The plateau surface was badly crevassed and swathed in sastrugi—hard waves formed by wind on a snow surface—which jerked the sleds and threatened to break the men's skis. When conditions made skiing impossible, they walked instead. All the while, wind nipped at their faces, turning their breath into cakes of ice that clung to their beards, and left their noses white with frostbite.

Christmas Day was also William Lashly's 44th birthday, and he "celebrated" by plunging into another crevasse. After a march of 17 miles, the men enjoyed a special Christmas hoosh of pemmican, biscuits, and horse meat, flavored with onion and curry powder. This was followed by a chocolate hoosh, plum pudding, cocoa with raisins, and finally a dessert of caramels and ginger. With gloriously full stomachs, everyone settled down for a splendid sleep.

THE FINAL FIVE

SCOTT CHOOSES HIS POLAR TEAM

The marching continued at a steady pace, and by December 31, they had caught up with Shackleton's timings. Now, just 180 miles from the Pole, Scott laid the first plateau depot (3 Degree Depot) and ordered Teddy Evans's team to leave their skis there.

Now that there was less weight to haul, Edgar "Taff" Evans began converting both 12 ft. sleds into 10 ft. sleds. As he made his adjustments, he cut his hand badly. Knowing that Scott would not take an injured man to the Pole, he carefully concealed his injury.

Three days later, Scott announced the names of the lucky men who would get a shot at the Pole. Departing from his original plan, he chose four men instead of three. They were Bill Wilson, Birdie Bowers, Lawrence Oates, and—to his joy—Taff Evans. The last-minute change required modifications to rations and sleeping arrangements. What's more, Bowers would have no skis, having left them at the last depot. But, Scott calculated, these inconveniences would be a small price to pay for the extra pulling power.

Masking their disappointment with brave smiles and hearty handshakes, Teddy Evans, William Lashly, and Tom Crean turned for home on January 4.

As the polar party crept south, with no trace of the Norwegians to be found, it was only the near certainty of reaching the Pole first that kept their shattered bodies going. All the hurdles that nature continued to throw in their path were bearable now that the Pole was within touching distance.

SO CLOSE AND YET . . .

APPROACHING THE POLE

At last, on January 15, the men found themselves just two long marches from the Pole.

"It is wonderful," wrote Scott. "It ought to be a certain thing now."

The next day they were off to a flying start, covering over 7.5 miles in the morning. Their spirits soared as they set off again after lunch. This time tomorrow the Pole would quite literally be within their sights.

But an hour or two into the afternoon march, the mood shifted abruptly. Something in the far distance had caught Bowers's eagle eyes. Was that a cairn poking up from the flat, white expanse?

The thought made everyone uneasy but, ever the optimist, Bowers insisted it must be a natural phenomenon—a large sastruga or something similar. Doing their best to believe him, the men crunched onward. But it was not long before hope turned to gut-wrenching despair.

Straining his eyes, Bowers declared he could now see a black speck ahead. And, as they gained on it, they saw it was a marker flag tied to a pole. Nearby were the remains of a camp, surrounded by sled and ski tracks and countless imprints of busy dog paws.

"This told us the whole story," a distraught Scott wrote that evening. "It is a terrible disappointment, and I am very sorry for my loyal companions . . . all the day dreams must go."

AT THE END OF THE EARTH

ARRIVING AT THE SOUTH POLE

Nobody slept much that night, but the next day, January 17, 1912, they somehow mustered the energy to drag themselves and their sled the final desperate miles to their goal. With the men sapped of hope and drained of adrenaline, the -22°F temperature and gusting headwind hit them harder than ever. It was, Wilson wrote, "a very bitter day."

That night they camped as close to the Pole as possible, with the intention of checking and perfecting their measurements the next day. Wrapped in his sleeping bag, pencil gripped in his icy fingers, Scott poured his despair into his trusty diary: "Great God!" he exclaimed, "this is an awful place."

The following morning, they began checking and rechecking their position with their instruments. Deciding that they were just over 3 miles from the Pole, they headed south once more.

They had not gone far when they came across a small tent topped with a Norwegian flag. Inside were a few items of equipment and a note from Roald Amundsen:

> *Dear Captain Scott,*
> *As you are probably the first to reach this area after us, I will ask you kindly to forward this letter to King Haakon VII. If you can use any of the articles left in the tent please do not hesitate to do so. With kind regards.*
> *I wish you a safe return.*
> *Yours Truly*
> *Roald Amundsen*

Another note gave the names of the five Norwegians who had made it to the Pole. It was dated December 16, 1911—one month and one day before the British arrival.

Numb with cold and bitter disappointment, there was nothing the men could do but complete the task they'd risked their lives to accomplish.

Continuing to the patch of snow they had calculated to be the South Pole, the men built a cairn, raised their Union Jack flag, and photographed themselves—their grim faces etched with dismay.

"Well," Scott wrote that evening, "we have turned our back now on the goal of our ambition with sore feelings and must face our 800 miles of solid dragging!"

THE RETURN JOURNEY

THE LONG WALK HOME

With heavy steps and even heavier hearts, the men began to retrace their path. Now that their polar dream had melted away, it was harder than ever to ignore the savage hunger that gripped their growling stomachs. In truth—because they were burning more energy than their meager rations provided—they were slowly starving.

Bit by bit, their bodies were breaking down. Worst hit was Evans, whose injured hand was causing him trouble. Then came Oates, whose feet and face were succumbing to frostbite. By February, Evans's fingernails had started to drop off and Oates's big toe had turned black. Meanwhile, Wilson was suffering from sore eyes and a strained leg tendon, Scott had injured his shoulder, and even the hardy Bowers was feeling the cold.

All the while, as winter began to close in, falling temperatures, blizzards, gales, and a surface covering of sticky ice crystals made dragging hard and slow.

By February 4, Bowers had retrieved his skis and they were nearly back at the Beardmore Glacier. But that day, things took a turn for the worse when Evans fell down a crevasse and struck his head. Already suffering with his festering hand, his health spiraled alarmingly downward. Usually steady, strong, and reliable, he became, in Scott's words, "dull and incapable."

As the team navigated the torturous maze of the glacier, Evans grew worse by the day. A brief pause for Wilson to collect rock samples provided a welcome rest, but everyone knew that stopping any longer to nurse a sick teammate would mean death for them all.

By February 17, the men were short on rations and still a day's march from the Lower Glacier Depot. Anxious to get going, Scott was dismayed when Evans stopped pulling the sled. Trailing slowly behind his teammates, he rapidly disappeared from sight.

When Scott returned to look for him after lunch, he found him on his knees in the snow, disheveled and "with a wild look in his eyes." Evans died quietly that night, surrounded by his teammates.

As terrible as it was to lose a companion in this way, Scott hoped that without Evans to slow them down, and with the glacier behind them, they might finally pick up the pace. They needed to travel an average of 11 miles per day across the Barrier if they were to make it home alive. It was a reasonable goal but, yet again, events conspired against them.

THE BITTER END

THE TEAM'S FINAL DAYS

Winter was closing in fast. Temperatures continued to fall, strong winds had extinguished the men's outbound tracks, and the "impossible friction" of the barrier surface slowed them to a sluggish pace.

As a final insult, just when they needed fuel more than ever, the men discovered that the kerosene cans left at the depots were running low.

With supplies dwindling, they had to use the bare minimum—meaning fewer hot drinks and some very cold, or even frozen, meals.

Most worryingly, Oates was starting to fail. His frostbitten and gangrenous feet were now in a "wretched condition" and, by March 12, he was hardly pulling the sled at all. Now a fatal hindrance rather than a help, Scott wondered how long his friend would last. The answer came a few days later—on or around March 17—which also happened to be Oates's 32nd birthday.

As a blizzard whipped around their tent, the men shivered in their sleeping bags. Summoning all his strength, Oates made his way to the tent opening. "I am just going outside," he told the others, "and may be some time." He was never seen again.

"We knew that poor Oates was walking to his death, but though we tried to dissuade him, we knew it was the act of a brave man," wrote Scott.

With just three of them left, they struggled on the next day. Their goal was to get to One Ton Depot, where vital food and fuel awaited them. That evening, Scott discovered that his right foot was badly frostbitten.

By the night of March 19, they were within 11 miles of the depot. In their ration bags they had a day's worth of fuel and food for two days. Tantalizingly close to salvation, the weather now unleashed its very worst on them. A severe blizzard trapped them in their tents. Stretching out their supplies, they waited for it to pass. But day after day, the storm kept raging and, hour by hour, the men grew weaker and weaker. On Thursday, March 29, Scott wrote a short entry in his diary. It was to be his last:

I do not think we can hope for any better things now. We shall stick it out to the end, but we are getting weaker, of course, and the end cannot be far. It seems a pity, but I do not think I can write more.
R. Scott

For God's sake look after our people.

SCOTT'S LEGACY

THE AFTERMATH

News of the tragedy did not reach Britain until February 1913. Memorial services were held across the country, including a magnificent one at St. Paul's Cathedral in London. Ordinary men and women got to work raising enough money to look after the dead men's families, settle the expedition's debts, and even build the Scott Polar Research Institute in Cambridge—a center dedicated to researching the polar regions, which still exists today.

Hailed as national treasures, Scott and his fellow explorers were celebrated as models of bravery, resilience, and strength.

But in the decades that followed, some cast doubt on Scott's heroic status. Comparing him harshly with his rival Roald Amundsen, they questioned his leadership and criticized his decision-making.

In recent years, the wheel has turned again. Even heroes make mistakes, commentators argue, especially when they are under crippling pressure in extreme environments. Scott was no different.

Whatever Scott's failings, arguments about them are a noisy distraction from something far more important: his expedition's priceless scientific record. When the *Terra Nova* returned from Antarctica, it carried with it a unique harvest of data and samples.

COMPASS, THERMOMETER, BAROMETER, AND SUN COMPASS

Scott and his team continued to make weather observations throughout their trek to the South Pole. Their meteorological log was found on a sled buried in the snow, near the tent where the bodies of Scott, Wilson, and Bowers were found.

WILSON'S NOTEBOOK

Bill Wilson filled notebooks with drawings and notes on Antarctic wildlife throughout the expedition.

THREE EMPEROR PENGUIN EGGS

Collected by Bowers, Cherry-Garrard, and Wilson during "The Worst Journey in the World"

SPINY ICEFISH

(Chaenodraco wilsoni)

Named after Wilson

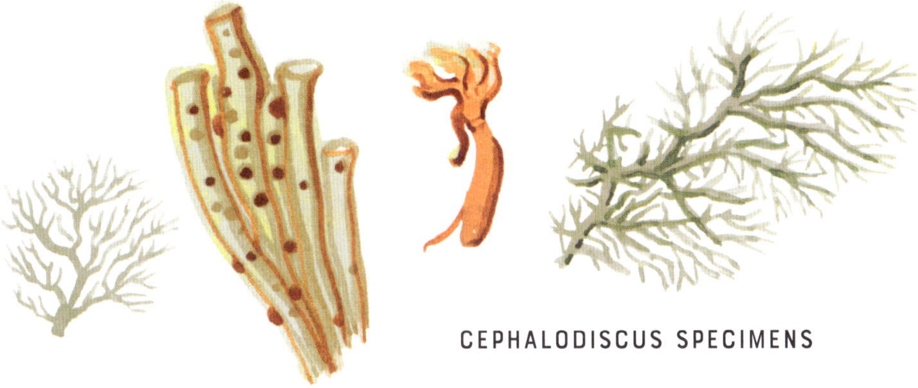

CEPHALODISCUS SPECIMENS

BRITTLE STAR SPECIMEN

These included thousands of animal and plant specimens—around 400 of which were new to science; thousands of rocks and fossils that have helped explain the history of the Antarctic continent; the longest unbroken record of weather collected in the early twentieth century; meticulous and groundbreaking studies of Antarctic wildlife; exquisitely detailed surveys of Antarctic ice; and data on ocean temperatures and currents.

All of their precious findings were pored over by scientists back in the UK. Over 100 years later, experts today continue to use the expedition's data to assess how Antarctica has changed over the years, and to understand how human activity is impacting the natural world.

Following in the footsteps of Scott and his team, this research helps us make informed decisions about how we treat our planet, and how we tackle climate change. For the man who called science "the rock foundation of all effort," there is surely no better legacy.

ANTARCTIC ISOPOD

FOSSIL OF GLOSSOPTERIS

Collected by Bill Wilson on the polar team's return down the Beardmore Glacier. Glossopteris is an extinct plant that once grew in India, Africa, New Zealand, Australia, and South America. This incredible fossil—the first of its kind to be found in Antarctica—provided vital evidence that Antarctica had once been part of the supercontinent Gondwana.

SADDLEBACK PLUNDERFISH

(Pogonophryne scotti)

Named after Scott

ANTARCTICA TODAY

Well over a century has passed since Amundsen, Scott, and their eight companions reached the South Pole. During that time, many others have followed in their wake—traveling by foot, sled, plane, and even by tractor!

Now, instead of a bare patch of wind-whipped snow and ice, visitors find a sign recording the names of the two explorers and the dates of their arrival—just thirty-three days apart.

They also find the Amundsen–Scott South Pole Station: one of over fifty scientific research stations scattered across Antarctica. These stations are operated by a host of international scientists dedicated to studying Antarctica—its climate, geology, glaciers, sea ice, ocean currents, wildlife, and much more.

Why is this work so important? Because, although Antarctica may seem remote, what happens in this great frozen wilderness affects us all—influencing global weather, climate, sea levels, and precious ecosystems.

So, understanding and protecting Antarctica is key to understanding and protecting our entire planet. In an age of growing populations and rising temperatures, a new race has begun, one that we must run together: the race to protect and preserve this extraordinary—and extraordinarily important—continent for countless centuries to come.

EARTH'S FRIDGE

Antarctica acts as Earth's refrigerator, reflecting the sun's energy from its bright, white surface, helping keep temperatures cool.

RISING TEMPERATURES

The average annual temperature of the Antarctic Peninsula rose by up to 5.8°F in the second half of the 20th century. Since the 1950s, a total of 9,650 mi^2 of ice shelf has been lost from around the peninsula.

ICE SHEETS

Antarctica is covered by two major areas of ice, divided by the Transantarctic Mountains: the East and West Antarctic Ice Sheets. These sheets are up to 15,750 ft. thick and they contain 60% of the world's total fresh water.

FLAGS AT THE POLE

Not far from where a Norwegian flag once marked victory, twelve flags now stand around the Ceremonial South Pole—one for each nation that signed the original Antarctic Treaty in 1959, agreeing to keep Antarctica a peaceful place of scientific investigation and collaboration.

FROZEN IN TIME

Ice sheets form from layers of snow that have built up and compacted into ice over millions of years. Scientists drill ice cores—thick columns of ice—which contain information about the climate of the distant past and how it has changed over time.

WILDLIFE WATCHING

Today, scientists use technology including tracking devices, satellites, and even robots to study animals, such as penguins, and monitor the impact that changes to the climate and environment are having on them.

ICE SHELVES

Much of Antarctica's coastline is fringed by ice shelves, which are thick plates of floating ice. They are formed when land ice flows out into the sea. The Ross Ice Shelf (formerly known as The Great Ice Barrier) is the largest ice shelf in Antarctica. Some areas are over 2,000 ft. thick and its surface is roughly the size of Texas.

SEA ICE

In winter, over half of the Southern Ocean freezes over. This sea ice helps drive important ocean currents that carry vital heat, oxygen, carbon, and nutrients around the globe.

Turn the book around to read the other side of the story!

1926, AMUNDSEN FLIES OVER THE NORTH POLE

Six hundred feet up in the air, Amundsen clasped Wisting's hand. Nothing was said—nothing needed to be said. Both Poles. They had done it!

In 1928, Amundsen set out on one last mission, this time to search for Umberto Nobile and his crew, whose airship, the *Italia*, had crashed north of Svalbard, a Norwegian archipelago in the Arctic Ocean. Amundsen set off in a flying boat with five companions, but none of them were ever seen again.

For the man nicknamed "The Last of the Vikings," Amundsen's death was a fitting exit.

"The end, no doubt, was as he himself would have wished it," Lincoln Ellsworth told the world in a heartfelt speech. "For Amundsen often told me that he wanted to die in action."

Almost 100 years later, Amundsen continues to be remembered in Norway and around the world as one of the greatest figures of the so-called "Heroic Age" of Antarctic Exploration—and one of the greatest explorers of all time.

But his gift to the world was far greater than a thrilling tale of danger and derring-do. Not only did he blaze a trail into the heart of Earth's most mysterious continent, but he also opened up new frontiers for science and exploration.

Above all, though, he showed humankind what we can achieve through determination, teamwork, and a willingness to learn from our own, and others', experiences.

1928, AMUNDSEN TAKES OFF ON HIS FINAL FLIGHT

AMUNDSEN'S NORWEGIAN FLAG

Amundsen took the same Norwegian flag with him on four of his major expeditions and had it embroidered to commemorate each occasion: Northwest Passage 1903–1906, South Pole, 12-14-1911, Northeast Passage 1918–1920, North Pole 5-13-1927.

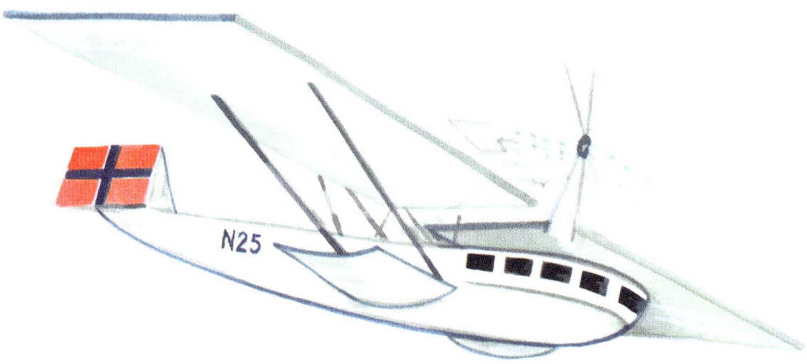

1925, AMUNDSEN ATTEMPTS TO FLY TO THE NORTH POLE IN A FLYING BOAT

FLYING NORTH

AMUNDSEN'S LATER ADVENTURES

It would be seven long years before Amundsen returned to polar climes. With moneymaking opportunities rolling in, he postponed his long-planned expedition to the Arctic. But, more at ease on desolate icy plains than in crowded halls, he found the endless cycle of talks and dinners tiresome.

The outbreak of World War I in 1914 caused further delays, but finally, in July 1918, Amundsen embarked on his long-awaited Arctic adventure. But this time, things did not go to plan.

Despite all the expertise on board, the expedition was dogged with difficulty and disaster. The hapless Amundsen broke his arm, nearly died of carbon monoxide poisoning, and was even attacked by a polar bear.

Worst of all, a year into the expedition, two team members went missing and were never seen again. They never came close to reaching the North Pole.

Eventually, Amundsen abandoned the scheme in favor of something even more daring. In 1925, he attempted to fly to the North Pole alongside the American explorer Lincoln Ellsworth and four others, in two "flying boats." The mission ultimately failed, but they did make it further north than any plane had before them.

A year later, with Ellsworth, Oscar Wisting, and Italian aeronautical engineer Umberto Nobile, Amundsen flew an airship, the *Norge*, steadily across the North Pole!

1918, EXPLORING THE NORTHEAST PASSAGE
The ship *Maud* was specially built for Amundsen's expedition to the Arctic and named after the Norwegian Queen Maud.

1919, ATTACKED BY POLAR BEAR
The polar bear was startled by one of the crew's dogs and attacked to protect her cub. Amundsen barely escaped with his life.

The very next day, newspaper headlines around the world proclaimed:

AMUNDSEN REACHES THE SOUTH POLE!
Norwegian Explorer Sends Word
of His Success From Tasmania.
No News From Capt. Scott.

The story was out, and Amundsen now began making the most of his triumph. He gave interviews, wrote a book, and embarked on a worldwide lecture tour. Everyone wanted to hear about his team's daring adventures in the world's most desolate place.

A VICTORIOUS RETURN

HOMEWARD BOUND

The five men, and just eleven dogs, returned to the Bay of Whales on January 26, 1912. The journey home had been cold, hard, and dangerous—but somehow they had come through unscathed.

For Amundsen and his team, it was clear their success owed everything to hard work and careful planning. Luck had nothing to do with it.

But there was little time for self-congratulation. They needed to tell the world what they had achieved. The race would not be truly won until the telegram announcing their victory had been safely dispatched.

The *Fram* had returned to the Bay of Whales earlier that month. So, wasting no time, Amundsen and the men began packing their bags. They loaded the remaining twenty-nine dogs and only their most precious equipment onto the ship before setting sail for Hobart, Tasmania, on January 30.

When they arrived just over a month later, on March 7, Amundsen headed swiftly ashore clutching his telegram briefcase.

The flag had been raised, but the work was not over quite yet. It was impossible, Amundsen freely admitted, to work out the exact spot at which the South Pole lay with the instruments and time they had at hand. But he would try his best to get as close as he could.

The men spent three days circling the Pole and taking measurements. When they were done, Amundsen concluded that the Pole was at a slightly different location. So, on December 17, they pitched a small tent at the "actual Pole," with a Norwegian flag attached to the top.

Naming the tent "Polheim"—Home at the Pole—Amundsen left a few items inside: letters to King Haakon of Norway and Captain Scott recording their historic arrival at the Pole; a few items of clothing; and some navigational instruments.

Then, with a final farewell to Polheim and their flag, they turned northward.

CROSSING THE FINISH LINE

ARRIVAL AT THE SOUTH POLE

The next morning brought good weather, and the men set off as soon as possible. Advancing steadily across the endless flat plain, they barely exchanged a word.

Then, at 3pm, the word "Halt!" rang out. The sled-meters showed they had completed the full distance to the Pole.

Around them stretched snow—crisp, white, and untouched. They had done it. First to the Pole! With hearty handshakes and the widest grins, the smiling men congratulated one another.

Together, five frostbitten fists raised a fluttering Norwegian flag in the air and planted it in the ground. Pride and affection shone in each man's eyes.

Tantalizingly, they were now less than 97 miles from the Pole. Would they make it there alive? And, if so, would they get there first?

The strain gnawed away at them. In one dreadful moment, Bjaaland thought he saw sleds on the horizon. But, after a few moments of panic, he admitted his imagination must be playing tricks.

By now the men's faces were covered in painful frost-sores, and they were exhausted. Had they been sledding on the Barrier it would have been tough enough, but high up on the Polar Plateau—where there was less oxygen to breathe—every step was a struggle.

To make matters worse, the dogs were worn out too—thinner, slower, and ravenously hungry.

Nevertheless, there was hope in the air. The crevasses, neckbreaking sastrugi, and gale-force winds had disappeared, and the sun had even come out.

On the night of December 13—with just one march to go—the men readied their Norwegian flag and settled down to sleep as best they could.

"I was awake several times in the night," wrote Amundsen, "and had the same feeling that I can remember as a little boy on the night before Christmas."

THE LAST LEG

JOURNEY ACROSS THE POLAR PLATEAU

The storm continued, pummeling the men with whirling snow. At times, the air was so thick with flying crystals that they couldn't see the dogs ahead of their sleds. They were running blind over perilous ground. But there was no time to wait for the weather to clear.

A few days later, they reached a gleaming frozen lake. Beneath its polished surface lay a false floor of ice. And, beneath that, lurked a network of crevasses. Time after time the dogs and men plunged through the ice. They called this nightmarish place the "Devil's Ballroom," and Amundsen declared it the most unpleasant march of the whole trip.

But such obstacles served only to spur the men on—that and the fear of being beaten by the British.

A handful of days later, they passed the "furthest south" record—set by explorer Ernest Shackleton in 1909. "No other moment of the whole trip affected me like this," Amundsen later wrote.

The dogs had done all that Amundsen could have hoped for—and more. So it was with great sadness that he now ordered twenty-four of them to be shot. This had always been part of his master plan. The dead dogs would provide much-needed food for the rest of the pack and the men. What's more, their fresh meat would ward off scurvy—a disease caused by a severe vitamin C deficiency. This was a trick that Amundsen had learned on his first trip to Antarctica.

Naturally, everyone was anxious to leave the camp, which they had nicknamed "The Butcher's Shop." But a raging blizzard trapped them in their tents for four frustrating days. Here they lay—restless and struggling to breathe in the thin air.

After dividing the remaining dogs into three teams and repacking the sleds, they eventually set off again on November 25.

WHICH WAY UP?

SEARCHING FOR A GLACIER

On November 17, the glittering pinnacles of the Transantarctic Mountains loomed before them. Although they looked like a fairytale, Amundsen knew that if he could not find a way through them, they would spell the end of his dreams.

But luck was on his side. After searching for a few days, he found what he needed: a glacier 30 miles long stretching steeply up to the Polar Plateau. He called it the Axel Heiberg Glacier, in honor of one of his sponsors.

With the rumble of avalanches echoing around them, and chasms and crevasses at every turn, the men and dogs battled their way up the glacier. On some of the steepest slopes, they had to use two dog teams per sled and even do some hauling themselves. Incredibly, after just four days, they reached the edge of the Polar Plateau. Numb with exhaustion, they dragged themselves into their tents for a rest.

Although the temperature was now warmer, the Barrier had other booby traps in store. Thick fog, blinding blizzards, and vast crevasse fields hampered progress, with sleds and men at constant danger of tumbling into icy voids.

At one stage, Bjaaland's sled disappeared into a yawning chasm. Jumping off, in the nick of time, he eventually managed to haul it out with the help of his teammates. Not long afterward, Wisting plummeted into another crevasse—saving himself from certain death by clinging to the sides.

"There was no need to look for crevasses," Amundsen commented wryly, "there was literally nothing else to be seen."

All this aside, the team still managed to cover more than 17 miles a day. Building snow beacons every few miles to mark their route, they reached their final depot on November 4. From here onward, they would be plunging into the unknown.

ICY TRAPS

Antarctica's ice is always on the move. As a result, it often splits apart to form crevasses. These are cracks in the ice that can be hundreds of feet deep, hundreds of feet across, and miles long. Crevasses are often hidden under a layer of snow—making them even more treacherous!

RACING SOUTH

SOUTHERN JOURNEY TO THE POLE

Weeks later, on October 19, the men set off again —this time without Johansen. Amundsen's convoy now consisted of: Olav Bjaaland, Helmer Hanssen, Oscar Wisting, and Sverre Hassel; fifty-two dogs; and four sleds loaded with 770 lb. of gear.

Their journey would involve three stages. Firstly, the men would cross the Great Ice Barrier. Secondly, they would ascend to nearly 9,800 ft. from the Barrier to the high Polar Plateau, and finally, they would cross the Plateau to the South Pole.

Even though Amundsen was almost 60 miles closer to the Pole than Captain Scott, he had one huge disadvantage. Unlike the British, who were retracing the footsteps of two previous expeditions, the Norwegians were heading into the unknown. Nobody had ever traveled beyond their final depot. Whatever obstacles lay between there and the Pole, Amundsen had to trust he would find a way around them.

With barely a backward glance, Amundsen dashed back to Framheim—leaving two of his badly frostbitten teammates trailing in his wake. They arrived back many hours after their leader, exhausted and on the verge of collapse.

The next morning, Hjalmar Johansen—the oldest and most experienced member of the team—openly criticized Amundsen's leadership. An enraged Amundsen was having none of it. "On our journey south, there must be no critical elements," he wrote in his diary. "Especially, when they come from an old polar explorer like him, they become doubly dangerous."

A FALSE START

AMUNDSEN MAKES A NEAR FATAL MISTAKE

The men spent the winter perfecting their equipment and fine-tuning their plans to reach the Pole. By the time the sun reappeared in August, they were well-prepared, well-rested, and raring to go.

Amundsen, in particular, was anxious to set off as soon as the temperatures were bearable.

Although he had originally planned to wait for summer to arrive, he was determined to have a head start on Scott and get going sooner. He had staked everything—his reputation, his fortune, and his pride—on this race. He simply could not afford to lose.

"The thought of the English gave him no peace," teammate Sverre Hassel wrote in his diary. "If we were not the first at the South Pole, you might just as well stay at home."

As each day passed, the tension mounted and Amundsen's nerves became increasingly frayed. Finally, the temperatures on the thermometers began to rise, and on September 8, they departed.

But they had blinked too soon. Three days into their journey, the temperature plunged to -67°F. The compasses froze, the men's feet became frostbitten, and the dogs' paws began to bleed. One dog dropped dead in its tracks and several more froze to death. There was only one thing to do: turn around.

Although eight dogs had died from the cold and exhaustion in the process, Amundsen knew from experience that they were by far the safest and most efficient way of traveling over treacherous polar terrain. His mind boggled at Scott's decision to rely on heavy and unwieldy ponies.

"If a dog falls into a crevasse there is no great harm done; a tug at his harness and he is out again," he wrote. "But it is another matter with a pony."

By the time the team arrived back at base, the *Fram* had long since left for Buenos Aires, Argentina, where it would overwinter.

Tucked safely inside Framheim, with their dogs hunkering down in tents outside, the nine Norwegians watched as the flaming red sun slipped below Antarctica's horizon and disappeared altogether. They would not see it again for four long months.

GET SET . . .

PREPARING TO RACE

The men were not due to leave for the Pole until September 1911 at the earliest—once the Antarctic winter had passed. But, when the time came, the dog sleds would not be able to carry everything the team needed to get there and back. So, Amundsen decided to drop food and fuel supplies along the route in advance, at clearly marked points, called "depots." He had two months in which to do this, before the perilous polar winter arrived—plunging them into perpetual night.

The first depot-laying expedition left on February 10, 1911. To everyone's delight, the dogs set off at a rattling pace, covering a total of 106 miles in just six days. Amundsen was thrilled with how smoothly everything went.

By the time they had finished a few weeks later, the men had dropped three tons of supplies at three depots. They had also gained precious experience with the dogs, equipment, and the merciless Antarctic environment.

A CHANCE ENCOUNTER

WHEN *FRAM* MET *TERRA NOVA*

The crew were still unloading the *Fram* on February 4, when they received a surprise visit. It was from none other than Scott's ship, the *Terra Nova*. The ship's Captain, Lieutenant Campbell, told Amundsen that he had been sent eastward by Scott to explore King Edward VII Land—an Antarctic peninsula not far from the Bay of Whales.

If either side found the meeting awkward, nobody let on. The two rival parties even had lunch together aboard the *Terra Nova*. "We spent a couple of very agreeable hours together," Amundsen breezily recalled.

But Amundsen had no time to ponder the bizarre encounter and, just six days later, he embarked on the next stage of his plan.

As the sleds ran back and forth, the carpenters began building the wooden hut that would serve as the men's living quarters. Snug, cozy, and meticulously clean, they fondly christened it "Framheim"—Home of the *Fram*.

Over the course of the next few months, the nine men who made up the shore party would turn their base into a mini village: putting up tents for the dogs and hollowing out hobbit-like workshops and passages under the snow drifts. There was even an underground steam bath!

HOME OF THE *FRAM*

SETTING UP CAMP IN ANTARCTICA

The voyage south took four monotonous months. So, when the little ship cruised quickly and safely through the Antarctic pack ice into open water in January 1911, everyone aboard heaved a heartfelt sigh of relief.

Not long afterward, the *Fram* reached her destination: the Bay of Whales. Amundsen had identified this inlet on Antarctica's Great Ice Barrier as an ideal place to land. It had many advantages: it was relatively easy to sail to; it was a respectable distance from Captain Scott's hut on Ross Island—around 400 miles away; and, most importantly, it was 60 miles closer to the South Pole than the British base.

Tethering the ship to the ice, the men searched for a suitable place to set up camp. It was not long before they had settled on a sheltered spot just 2.5 miles in from the Barrier edge. Wasting no time, the dogs and men began ferrying 900 boxes of gear from the *Fram* to their new home.

The *Fram* was built for the legendary Norwegian polar explorer Fridtjof Nansen, and had already been on two Arctic expeditions. The ship was specially designed to handle the pressures of sea ice.

As well as two years' worth of food, fuel, and equipment, the ship's cargo included a library of over 3,000 books, among other luxuries.

The crew were greatly outnumbered by animals. At the start of the voyage there were ninety-seven Greenland dogs on board and by the time the *Fram* arrived in Antarctica there were 116 dogs, as several dogs had pups along the way!

Everyone enjoyed having the dogs on board but they weren't the easiest shipmates. As well as cleaning up endless piles of dog poop, the men had to stop mass dog brawls from breaking out. Other animal crew members included four pigs, six carrier pigeons, and one canary.

A SNEAKY START

THE *FRAM* TRAVELS SOUTH

The summer sun was sinking below the horizon when the *Fram* set sail on August 10, 1910. As they watched the Norwegian shoreline disappear into the darkness, only a handful of the nineteen men on board knew their real destination. The rest would find out a whole month later, when the ship stopped in Madeira to take on fresh supplies.

As the crew prepared to leave the island on September 9, Amundsen called everyone onto the deck and boldly explained his true intentions. All-around astonishment soon turned to feverish excitement and, "before I had finished," Amundsen later recalled, "they were all bright with smiles."

Now that the crew knew the truth, it was time to tell the world. Carefully crafted letters were sent out to explain Amundsen's momentous decision. The most important of these were addressed to his mentor and fellow explorer Fridtjof Nansen, King Haakon VII of Norway, and the newspapers. On October 5, a brisk telegram was dispatched to Captain Scott informing him of Amundsen's Antarctic detour.

As the world came to grips with the exciting plot twist, the *Fram* continued on its long voyage south. It would not drop anchor again until it reached Antarctica.

BORROWED WISDOM

During his Northwest Passage expedition, Amundsen had spent two winters living among the Netsilik Inuit on King William Island in northern Canada. While there, he learned precious polar survival skills from his new neighbors, including how to hunt seals and make igloos. He was particularly impressed by their excellent reindeer skin clothing and footgear, and their skillful use of sled dogs to travel over the ice. Amundsen drew heavily on the Inuit's expert knowledge and skills when planning and packing for the expedition to Antarctica.

REINDEER SKIN ANORAK

REINDEER SKIN PANTS

KEEPING WARM

Amundsen had reindeer skin outfits made for himself and his crew, copying the patterns of Netsilik Inuit clothing. These designs were loose-fitting to reduce sweating—sweat is the last thing you want in polar conditions as it can freeze to your skin and clothing!

REINDEER SKIN MITTENS

DOGS AND SLEDS

Having learned how to drive sled dogs from the Inuit, Amundsen was convinced that they would lead him to victory at the South Pole. He couldn't understand why Scott was favoring ponies for his own expedition as dogs seemed a far better choice, in terms of both performance and practicality. Amundsen had also been taught some useful sledding tricks by the Inuit, including how to add a thin layer of ice to the bottom of the sled runners to make them glide more smoothly across the snow.

A CHANGE OF PLAN

SECRETLY HEADING SOUTH

Amundsen's new scheme was typically ambitious. Antarctica would merely be a "slight detour" on his way to the Arctic. After reaching the South Pole by dog sled and skis, he would hop back onto his ship —the *Fram*—and continue with his long-planned voyage to the frozen North. The money that would surely come flooding in after he reached the South Pole would pay for both expeditions.

There was, however, one major problem with this scheme. For some time, the famous British explorer, Captain Robert Falcon Scott, had been planning a high-profile expedition to Antarctica, which would include an attempt to reach the South Pole. He had announced his plans on September 13, 1909, to great international excitement.

Amundsen was confident he could beat Scott to the Pole, but his real fear was that when he publicly announced his new plan, chaos would ensue.

So, he plotted in secret, telling only his brother Leon and the *Fram*'s commander, Lieutenant Thorvald Nilsen. For the time being, the rest of the world would remain blissfully ignorant.

As Amundsen prepared for departure, his deception led to awkward questions. "Why is he sailing from Norway with Greenland dogs when he could pick them up in Alaska on the way?" people asked. "And why take materials for a hut when he'll be trapped in pack ice for five years?"

There was yet more awkwardness in March 1910, when Captain Scott visited Norway to trial a motor sled he planned to use in Antarctica. During his stay, Scott tried to get hold of Amundsen to discuss possible scientific cooperation between his expedition and the Norwegians' Arctic mission. Scott telephoned twice, but each time he was told that Amundsen was unavailable.

As a young man he had worked on Arctic seal hunting ships. At twenty-five, he had survived a harrowing winter on a ship trapped in the Antarctic sea ice. And, in 1906, he had become the first person to navigate the fabled Northwest Passage—a winding route through Canada's icy Arctic waters connecting the Atlantic and Pacific oceans.

His past expeditions had equipped Amundsen with the knowledge, skills, and drive to be a great polar explorer. He had been lucky enough to learn not only from experienced explorers, including his friend and mentor Frederick Cook, but also from the wisdom of Indigenous people who had been living in the frigid Arctic for centuries.

In search of the ultimate adventure, it was therefore only natural that Amundsen had set his sights on the North Pole: one of the last two glittering prizes left for explorers. Equipped with his wealth of experience and the steely determination of his Viking ancestors, Amundsen had been confident of success.

Daring and fraught with danger, his scheme involved freezing his ship into the Arctic pack ice and drifting slowly northward.

When the time was right, he would make a final dash to the Pole using skis and dog sleds.

But now the prize had been claimed and his Arctic hopes were ruined. Bruised but not beaten, Amundsen quickly came up with a radical solution. It was deceptively simple—and breathtakingly bold.

"Nothing else remained for me to do than try to solve the last great problem," he later wrote. "The South Pole."

NORTH OR SOUTH?

AMUNDSEN'S PLANS ARE SHATTERED

In September 1909, a bitter fight broke out between two American explorers. Both claimed to have become the first humans to set foot at the North Pole.

Watching quietly from the sidelines was the Norwegian explorer Roald Amundsen.

Although his cool and commanding exterior gave nothing away, inside was a man in turmoil.

For the past two years, Amundsen had been meticulously planning his own trip to discover the North Pole. It was a goal he had cherished for many years.

RACE TO THE SOUTH POLE

THE NORWEGIAN EXPEDITION

ALEXANDRA STEWART
SARAH WILKINS

t&h

GLOSSARY

Archipelago
A group of islands.

Aurora
A display of colorful light that sometimes appears in the night sky around the North and South Poles, also known as the northern and southern lights.

Cairn
A human-made mound used as a memorial or landmark. While usually made from stones, our polar explorers made cairns from snow as landmarks.

Ceremonial South Pole
An area close to the Geographic South Pole used for photo opportunities.

Crevasse
A deep opening or crack in the ice.

Depots
Places to store food, fuel, and equipment. Both polar teams laid depots along their routes to the Pole so they could stock up on the way.

Frostbite
An injury caused by exposure to extreme cold that most commonly affects extremities, such as toes, fingers, and noses. Symptoms can include pain, numbness, tingling, swelling, blistering, skin hardening, and discoloration.

Glacier
A large body of ice moving very slowly down a slope or valley.

Ice floe
A sheet of floating sea ice.

Ice sheets
Thick layers of ice that cover large areas of land.

Ice shelves
Thick platforms of ice that float on the ocean but are attached to land. They are formed when land ice flows out into the sea.

Mount Erebus
The world's most southern active volcano. Located on Ross Island, it is 12,447 ft. high.

Northwest Passage
An Arctic sea route between the islands of Northern Canada that connects the Atlantic and Pacific oceans.

Pack ice (The Pack)
Moving blocks of sea ice, measuring up to 6 miles across. Ships caught in pack ice can be crushed by it.

Polar Plateau
A desolate area in Antarctica's interior, covered by a thick ice sheet. It's around half the size of the US with an average altitude of 9,800 ft.

Sastrugi
(singular: sastruga) Long, wavelike ridges of hard snow, formed by the wind. They look like frozen sand dunes.

Scurvy
A disease caused by a severe vitamin C deficiency. Symptoms include tiredness, low moods, joint pain, and bleeding gums.

Sled-meter
An instrument that tracks distance traveled by counting the rotations of a wheel dragged behind a sled.

Snow blindness
A temporary eye condition caused by too much exposure to UV light from the sun's rays. It's like sunburn for your eyes and can be very painful.